Bee Pollen, Royal Jelly, Propolis and Honey

AN EXTRAORDINARY ENERGY AND HEALTH-PROMOTING ENSEMBLE

by RITA ELKINS, M.A.

Woodland Publishing
Pleasant Grove, UT

© 1996
Woodland Publishing, Inc.
P.O. Box 160
Pleasant Grove, UT 84062

CONTENTS

Introduction

Chapter 1

Chapter 2

Chapter 3

Chapter 4

Introduction

BEEHIVE PRODUCTS: POWER-PACKED HEALERS

Today, the quest for an all natural medicine that can counteract the ravages of time, heal injured or diseased tissue and supply energy promoting nutrients seems somewhat futile. While the search continues among medical practitioners, the honeybee continues to thrive in a world literally teeming with foods regarded throughout history as nothing less than miraculous.

Unquestionably, the world of the honeybee is a fascinating one. Since the beginning of time, man has venerated the honeybee and its hive products. For generations, people of all cultures have risked the sting of an outraged bee in their quest to obtain a precious honeycomb. The therapeutic and nutritive use of honey, royal jelly, propolis and bee pollen can be traced throughout the ages—a testament in and of itself of the immeasurably rich value of these substances.

Beehive products are among some of the most remarkable and versatile nutrients Mother Nature has to offer. Since history was first recorded, the beehive has been referred to as the true fountain of youth—a source of miracle healing, giver of the perfect food for man. Today, beehive products are enjoying a renaissance as more information surfaces supporting their superior value. In the midst of the new, modern-day plagues like cancer and AIDS, substances like Royal Jelly, Bee Pollen and Propolis are emerging as truly exceptional in their ability to protect against disease and aging. In addition, when taken in raw supplement form, these products can promote a significant increase in energy and stamina, two attributes desperately sought after in our high stress, malnourished society.

THE INCOMPARABLE VALUE OF LIVE FOODS FOR HUMAN HEALTH

Most of us are unaware that nutrients supplied by cooked fruits, vegetables and meats are not considered live in that their enzymes have been altered by exposure to high heat. Even taking a multivitamin that has been artificially synthesized cannot offer the superior nutrient array of a raw, live food. Beehive foods are just such superior food sources. They contain every nutrient required to sustain and support life in a pure, raw and unaltered form—a live form.

The pollen-making bee will fly vast distances to collect pollen and nectar, and a resinous substance called Propolis. These in combination with Royal Jelly and Honey provide life giving substances that can nourish, rejuvenate and heal. The human body requires 22 basic elements including vitamins, amino acids, hormone and enzymes. Bee Pollen is a raw, live, natural food that contains them all! Bee Pollen, along with other beehive products can provide the human body with an incomparable source of energy, promote longevity, and inhibit aging, fatigue and a whole host of other degenerative diseases. Bee Pollen, Propolis, Honey and Royal Jelly are nothing less than extraordinary in their ability to provide us with some of Nature's most superior foods and therapeutic agents. While most of us many be somewhat acquainted with the nutritional value of Bee Pollen and Honey, many of us do not fully appreciate the marvelous properties of Propolis and Royal Jelly.

Lets discuss Royal Jelly, Bee Pollen, Propolis, and Honey individually. While we don't want to get too technical, its important to understand the biochemistry of how these exceptional nutrients work in the human body to fully appreciate their marvelous value.

Chapter 1

ROYAL JELLY: CROWN JEWEL
OF THE BEEHIVE

It's safe to assume that a food fit for a queen bee would be beneficial for human beings. Royal Jelly is just such a food. Described as an incredibly rich, creamy, opalescent, white liquid, Royal Jelly is synthesized by the worker bees exclusively for the nourishment and cultivation of the queen bee. In other words, it is this remarkable material which miraculously transforms a common honey bee into a queen bee, extending its longevity from six weeks to five years. Considered the most precious gift of the hive, Royal Jelly is incomparable in its ability to enhance both physical and mental performance. Consider what it does for the queen bee:

*She measures 17 mm. and weighs 200 mg as compared to the 12 mm. and 125 mg. of the worker bee.

*Her sexual and reproductive capabilities are extremely impressive. She lays from 2,000 to 2,400 eggs every day weighing a total of 200 times her own body weight. During her lifetime, she will lay more than two million eggs, a feat that cannot be matched by any other creature on this planet.

*Even though she is hatched from the same egg as a honey bee, she will live from four to five years as compared to one to two months.[1]

Stated simply, Royal Jelly promotes longevity by helping to maintain health, beauty and youth. It is a potent, highly nutritional and natural food.

Royal Jelly: One of Nature's Best-Kept Secrets

Royal Jelly continues to baffle scientists. A highly complex compound, it has been extremely difficult for scientists to completely breakdown its components or to synthesize its compounds. No matter how Royal Jelly is poked, prodded and chemically analyzed, certain components of the substance still mystify even the most adept scientist. For this reason, duplicating what is thought to be the exact chemistry of Royal Jelly does not duplicate its effects in the human body. In other words, only honeybees can make Royal Jelly. Dr. Albert Saenz of the Pasteur Institute in Paris wrote:

"Numerous studies . . . demonstrate the existence of fractions in Royal jelly which correspond to 97 percent of the substance, plus an undermined fraction whose very presence could explain the remarkable and mysterious properties of Royal Jelly." He continues, " Here's yet another product of the beehive with a touch of the bee's magic in it. I suppose some day science will figure out what these unidentifiable elements are and some researcher will try to manufacture them. Until then, the only place to get these mystery nutrients is from the bees."[2]

Pheromones are among some of the elusive substances found in Royal Jelly.[3] As is the case with so many natural substances designed in specific formulas by Mother Nature, certain biochemical substances can only be found in nature. Don't be fooled by claims that exclusive, synthetic preparations can mimic the nutritional value of Royal Jelly or any other beehive product, for that matter. Not so.

Royal Jelly is rich in proteins and B-complex vitamins, particularly pantothenic acid (B5), which has been associated with reversing some of the effects of aging like the graying of hair.[4] While the chemical makeup of Royal Jelly may vary slightly according to its location, the United States Department of Agriculture has analyzed one gram of Royal Jelly to contain the following vitamin content discussed in the following section.

A Treasury of Active Compounds

Royal Jelly is a very complex mixture of compounds and contains roughly 12.34 percent protein, 5.46 percent lipids and 12 to 15 percent carbohydrates.[5] It is remarkably rich in natural hormones and B-vitamins. In addition, it contains an impressive array of 17 amino acids, including the eight essential amino acids, and is particularly rich in cystine, lysine and arginine. Royal Jelly is comprised of 16.1 percent of aspartic acid, which is absolutely essential for proper tissue growth and regeneration. Gelatin, another component of Royal Jelly is one of the primary precursors of collagen, a potent anti-aging compound that helps to keep our skin looking youthful while supporting our organs, glands and muscular systems.

Vitamin Content

Vitamin B1 (Thiamine)	1.5 to 7.4 mcg.
Vitamin B2 (Riboflavin)	5.3 to 10.0 mcg.
Vitamin B6 (Pyridoxine)	2.2 to 10.2 mcg.
Niacin (nicotinic acid)	91.0 to 149.0 mcg.
Pantothenic Acid	65.0 to 200.0 mcg.
Biotin	0.9 to 3.7 mcg.
Inositol	78.0 to 150.0 mcg.
Folic Acid	0.16 to 0.50 mcg.
Vitamin C	trace

Royal Jelly contains vital fatty acids, sugars, sterols, phosphorus compounds and acetylcholine. Acetylcholine is essential for the proper transmission of nerve impulses and the proper functioning of the endocrine system. A lack of acetylcholine can make us susceptible to a number of nerve disorders including Alzheimer's and Parkinson's disease, and Multiple Sclerosis. DNA and RNA, two nucleic acids found in Royal Jelly are referred to as the "very stuff of which life is made."[6]

CHARACTER: anti-bacterial, anti-viral, antibiotic, tonic, nutritive, anti-aging

BODY SYSTEMS TARGETED: Immune, Cardiovascular, Endocrine, Integumentary, Nervous, Reproductive, Cellular, Skeletal, Hepatic, Respiratory

FORMS: Royal Jelly may be purchased in a pure jelly-like material that should be kept frozen or refrigerated. It is also available in capsules, tablets, soft gels, and, in honey, chewables. Ideally, Royal Jelly is at its best when combined with other natural beehive products and complementary botanicals.

Dr. James f. Balch, M.D. a member of the American Board of Urology and American College of Surgeons has stated:

"When honey and pollen are combined and refined withing the young nurse bee, royal jelly is naturally created. This product must be combined with honey to preserve its potency. Royal Jelly spoils easily."

Obviously one very good way to present and preserve Royal Jelly is within its natural medium of pure honey. Taking freeze-dried (lyophilized) varieties of Royal Jelly is also highly recommended. Capsulized, freeze-dried varieties are excellent and more convenient to ingest than loose forms. Salves, ointments and cosmetics may also contain Royal Jelly.

SAFETY: Quality bee products should be purchased in order to obtain potent and pure varieties of any type of bee food or by-product. A relatively small percentage of the population may experience a laxative effect from Royal Jelly or Bee Pollen. Allergic reactions can happen but are quite rare. Some allergies are due to poor quality pollen, which has been gathered from commercially sprayed flowers or improperly cleaned, dried or stored. Anyone should begin using bee products slowly, in small amounts so as to ascertain if an allergic reaction will occur. No reported cases of Royal Jelly allergy were documented in a review of medical literature as of 1995 and only one case since then has been reported.[7]

Miraculous Rejuvenator

The notion that a veritable fountain of youth does indeed exist is intriguing to say the least. While we know that aging is inevitable, the aging process can be significantly slowed resulting in a kind of longevity and health many of us assume is unattainable. Researchers in Argentina have been working to scientifically document the ability of Royal Jelly to not only slow down tissue deterioration, but to reverse it as well. Consider Noel Johnson's story who experienced a rebirth of health at age 80. Keep in mind that in 1964 at age 65, he was refused life insurance due to a weak and damaged heart and was cautioned to dramatically restrict his physical activity or death could occur:

"I learned that bee products have more sex hormones than any other foods. . . old age and impotence go hand in hand. Bee products provide me with all necessary nutrients, plus the vital hormones which stimulate and nourish the sex glands of both men and women." In 1989, at age ninety, Johnson wrote a book called *The Living Proof...I Have Found the Fountain of Youth.* "I have made the products of the beehive the solid foundation of my nutritional program. Although I eat a large variety of whole foods, bee products are an unvarying part of my diet." Concerning his aged condition he stated, "I stripped down and looked in the mirror. All the classic signs of aging were there. I was 40 pounds overweight, with a bulging gut, dull eyes, slack unused muscles. I looked defeated . . . I knew I was doing everything wrong so I decided to teach myself to live right." Today, he holds the title of World's Senior Boxing Champion, often fighting much younger men to a standstill. His running schedule is grueling. Beginning with his first marathon in 1977, he usually brings home the gold medal in the Senior Division. What's his secret? Bee Products, Noel says. "I discovered the bee's gifts at age 70. These perfect live foods have restored my manhood, brought me to full vigor and sexual potency, and continue to nourish every cell in my body. I am improving in every way. I don't spend five cents on medicine." [8]

Hormonal Stimulant

The ability of Royal Jelly to stimulate and regulate endocrine function and hormonal secretion is another of its exceptional health benefits. "In manifestations of sexual involution, as well as in endocrine disorders, Royal Jelly in association with classic therapies accelerates the normal re-establishment of disturbed functions by means of its action on the adrenal cortex." [9]

Why Royal Jelly May Well Be the "Fountain of Youth"

James Devlin, Ph.D. writes:

"All of the legends surrounding the mysterious power and potency of royal jelly arise from these observations. Used both internally and externally, Royal Jelly was long believed to hold the secret of youth and beauty. Many observed that it revived the exhausted sexual powers of both men and women. Barren women and impotent men alike plotted to obtain it. Royal Jelly was once believed to confer eternal life. At the very least, it once was, and still is, regarded as a true Fountain of Youth that delivers rejuvenating and regenerative powers." [10]

Today, science has documented what were once thought to be the magical properties of Royal Jelly. The substance is nothing less than remarkable in its natural content of hormones, and other vital nutrients. In addition to being a superior source of vitamins, minerals and amino acids, Royal Jelly also includes gamma globulin and gelatinous collagen which are directly assimilated into the bloodstream. Dr. Alfred Vogel author of *The Nature Doctor* has written:

"Several years ago the newspapers reported that the Pope had recovered from a severe illness after his personal physician had prescribed royal jelly as a tonic for him. It was also reported that Dr. Paul Neihans, an eminent endocrinologist and specialist in live-cell therapy, concluded that royal jelly vitalized the glandular system in a similar way to an injection of fresh endocrine cells."[11]

Concerning the healing and regenerative properties of Royal Jelly, Dr. Steve Choi, C.N., a certified nutritionist had said:

"It [Royal Jelly] is reported to help in cell regeneration, inhibit the aging process, increase resistance to disease and help maintain skin tone and lustrous hair. It is also effective in treating different skin problems such as dry, scaly skin and acne."[12]

Dr. Albert Saenz of the Pasteur Institute in Paris puts is well when he says:

"Royal Jelly allows man to reestablish his biological balance and confront aging with optimism and serenity. Nature has created here in the extremely complex biological product, which is Royal Jelly, a genuine panacea for the aged and even, to put is simply, for the adult who aspires to push back the limits of his natural aging."[13]

Currently Royal Jelly is being studied by scientists along with five other traditional Chinese medicinal plants for its anti-aging properties.[14]

Energy Enhancer

Who among us doesn't need more energy? It's no secret that most of us live very stressful and hurried lives, eating on the run and sleeping poorly. Consequently, we continually battle constant fatigue and weariness. Dr. Eugene Oliveto highly recommends using Royal Jelly as a supplement for anyone who is experiencing chronic fatigue. "After taking it for about one month, these patients usually report that they feel more energetic."[15]

For centuries athletes have used beehive products to increase their endurance and stamina. Obviously, even for those of us who aren't planning to run any marathons, the nutritive components of bee foods are extremely desirable and often necessary to protect us against the foibles of fatigue, disease or aging. It is by boosting and supporting metabolic function that we obtain increased vigor and durability.

Some people refer to the ability of Royal Jelly to act as a metabolic catalyst as the R-Factor. This factor refers to the action of Royal Jelly which speeds up cellular functions and stimulates intracellular metabolic activities. Dr. P. Decourt believes that this R-Factor has a similar effect as a synthetic stimulant but with none of its detrimental side effects.[16] Therefore, while Royal Jelly is not technically a stimulant, it does cause an increase in energy and activity. Dr. Steve Choi, C.N. has said:

"Royal Jelly stimulates the adrenal glands and metabolism, giving more energy, rapid recovery from fatigue and enhanced sexual capabilities."[17]

Due to the increasing demands of family, work, school etc. Royal Jelly should be taken as a superior source of energy and endurance. The active compounds found in this extraordinary substance work to normalize and regulate all body functions and systems, resulting in increased vitality encompassing both physical and mental buoyancy.

Natural Antidepressant

Because it has the ability to mimic the stimulatory effect of amphetamines with no harmful side effects, Royal Jelly should be used in cases of anxiety, depression and even senility. Concerning this specific action, Dr. Albert Saenz has written: ". . . effectiveness has been demonstrated specifically in the aged, as well as in cases of senility in general . . . Cases of anxiety, depression, shock and senility all benefit from Royal Jelly treatment."[18]

Naturally, any substance that invigorates and boosts cellular regeneration would also benefit disorders related to brain neurochemistry. Today, scientists and physicians are just beginning to discover the profound link between physical and mental health.

"Royal" Weight Control

Speaking of metabolic functions, the burning of fat or thermogenesis, as it is technically known, can also be normalized by the chemical composition of Royal Jelly. In his book, *To Your Best Health*, Naturally, James A. Devlin, Ph.D. writes:

"In the mid-1960s, a Polish researcher discovered that Royal Jelly can normalize metabolic function. What this means is that Royal Jelly can prevent the regular user from becoming too fat or too skinny because of a metabolism that out of whack."[19]

Perhaps all of our diet-oriented efforts to slim down have been intrinsically flawed or mis-guided. The secret to maintaining a svelte figure may lie in the ability to nourish the body properly thereby inhibiting unnatural food cravings or the tendency to overeat.

Cholesterol Control

In a time when all of us are extremely concerned with cholesterol and lipid counts, Royal Jelly offers us another extraordinary benefit. Clinical tests conducted in 1995 found that serum lipids in mammals were significantly decreased after Royal Jelly was administered.[20] What this means is that taking Royal Jelly every day at recommended dosages can help to prevent atherosclerosis which can lead to heart attack and stroke. Scientists found that taking at least 100 mg. of Royal Jelly daily decreased total serum cholesterol levels by 14 percent and total serum lipids by 10 percent.[21]

Because lipoprotiens considerably increase with age, taking Royal Jelly before coronary heart disease has a chance to develop is the optimal way to enhance health and extend life.

The Great Health Recovery Aid

Any form of convalescence should be augmented by beehive products, especially Royal Jelly. Royal Jelly is capable of strengthening a body weakened by disease, malnutrition, trauma or surgery. Anyone who wants to get back on their feet as quickly as possible should make Royal Jelly, Bee Pollen and Propolis part of their nutritional regimen. As a member of this triad, Royal Jelly may be considered a complete therapeutic agent, providing excellent supplementation to diet and exercise.

THERAPEUTIC ACTIONS OF ROYAL JELLY

*helps to keep skin smooth, toned and elastic
*promotes sexual vitality and rejuvenation
*facilitates fertility and can reverse impotence
*stimulates the immune system to fight viral and bacterial infection
*regulates and balances hormones
*has a bacteriocidal action on bacteria like staph
*stimulates growth
*lowers blood lipids and cholesterol
*helps to regenerate bone growth
*builds tissue and muscles
*supports wound healing
*is hepato-protective (liver)
*increases vigor and physical strength
*provides extra physiological support during pregnancy and menopause
*helps to alleviate the pain of arthritis
*stimulates better memory and mental function
*has an antidepressive anti-anxiety effect
*can help to regulate weight
*rejuvenates the aged, sick or weak

PRIMARY APPLICATIONS OF ROYAL JELLY

Menopause Related Symptoms
Impotence
Infertility
Chronic Fatigue
Skin Blemishes and Wrinkles
Immune System Stimulant
Viral and Bacterial Infections
Endocrine System Disorders
Hormonal Imbalances

Coronary Artery Disease
High Cholesterol Levels
High Blood Pressure
Weight Control
Broken or Weak Bones
Retarded Growth
Bladder Infections
Wound Healing
Anemia
Inflammation
Liver Ailments
Cancer
Arthritis
Impaired Memory
Depression
Panic or Anxiety Attacks
Parkinson's Disease
Diabetes
Asthma
Anabolic Support (Athletic Abilities)
Weak or Tired Eyes
Arteriosclerosis
Atherosclerosis
Malnutrition
Mental Exhaustion
Mononucleosis
Ulcers
Eczema
Impetigo

How is Royal Jelly Harvested?

One might imagine how difficult it might be to collect Royal Jelly from worker bees. Because "milking" a bee is quite impractical, beekeepers have devised a system whereby Royal Jelly production is stepped up by removing the queen bee. When this occurs, Royal Jelly is deposited throughout the comb and can be harvested. For larger harvests, large colonies of queen bees are reared which results in a continuous harvest of Royal Jelly. Each queen chamber contains between 148 to 281 milligrams of Royal Jelly. To obtain 16 ounces or a pound of Royal Jelly, an average of 1,000 three-day old cells must be harvested in a very painstaking manner. A very small spoon or small vacuum is used to remove the Royal Jelly. At this point, the royal milk, as it is referred to, is quickly strained due to its delicate nature. Freeze-drying Royal Jelly when it is harvested helps to preserve its quality and potency. The process of cultivating, harvesting and making Royal Jelly consumer ready is very time consuming and requires skill and patience. The majority of the world's supply of Royal Jelly comes from China, where extraction techniques have been perfected.

Substances that Complement Royal Jelly

As mentioned earlier, taking Royal Jelly in a honey base or in combination with Bee Pollen or Propolis serves to potentiate its action. Another natural substance which makes an excellent partner with Royal Jelly is Panax Ginseng.

The marriage of Royal Jelly and Ginseng creates a potent blend of body rejuvenators and energizers. Panax Ginseng is a superior form of Ginseng and has been the subject of considerable scientific study around the world. It has impressive properties and can help to stimulate the central nervous system, thereby providing mental alertness, expanded energy and better cardiovascular health. Like Royal Jelly, it also works to lower blood cholesterol and protects cells from radiation damage.[22] Used for thousands of years to increase stamina and overall health, Ginseng provides Royal Jelly with the perfect mate.

NOTE: A high quality source of Royal Jelly is a pure and natural food which contains no caffeine, fillers, ephedra or artificial stimulants.

Royal Jelly Review

It's very difficult to thoroughly address all of the marvelous therapeutic properties of Royal Jelly. In attempting to summarize, it is vital to realize that the intricate interrelationship of the many complex compounds found in Royal Jelly works to preserve health and to sustain and extend life. Royal

Jelly is one of the extraordinary marvels of the honeybee kingdom and offers human beings a remarkable health promise. While the number of people who appreciate and use Royal Jelly is increasing, the majority of our population is unaware of its powerful properties.

To summarize, consider the following quote from a German medical doctor:

"The action of the active substance and nutrients contained in Royal Jelly takes place throughout the entire body. It acts to regulate all the functions of the human body. Considering all the investigations and observations made world wide regarding Royal Jelly, it is readily apparent that this is a powerful agent composed of hormones, nutrients, enzymes, and biocatalysts which starts up and revives the function of cells, the secretions of glands, the metabolism and blood circulation. . .To summarize, it is the interplay of all the complex factors present in Royal Jelly which works to preserve life and strength in the organism, which delays the aging, process, and which retains for as long as possible the elasticity of the mind, psychic buoyancy, and the youthful physical freshness of the body."[23]

Chapter 2

BEE POLLEN: FOOD FIT FOR THE GODS

Interestingly, while Bee Pollen has received a fair amount of attention of over the last few decades, many people still don't know exactly what it is. Technically, Pollen is the male seed of flowers. It can be looked at as the male sperm cells of flowering plants and is necessary for the plant to be fertilized.

Every kind of flower on this planet produces pollen, which is created in the stamen within the blossom itself. Bee pollen refers to pollen which is collected and stored by honey bees in their hives. Interestingly, while engaging in this industrious activity, honeybees pollinate more than 80 percent of green growing plants. They are very obviously a vital component of plant propagation. Bee Pollen is a food that has been universally praised for its impressive nutrient content and remarkable ability to provide energy.

A Brief History of Bee Pollen

Bee Pollen has been used as a food for centuries. Bees have produced nutritive foods for thousands of years, supplying sustenance for animals and eventually human beings. Bee Pollen has been considered a powerful healing agent, a source of regenerative power and for some ancients, the secret to eternal youth. As far back as 2735 B.C., Shen Nung, a Chinese emperor, compiled an impressive medical collection which discusses the merits of beehive products. This compilation is still referred to today, and ongoing scientific research continues to support many of its claims.

For millennia, humans have made good use of beehive products. Long before paper was invented, ancient people commemorated their veneration of the honeybee and beehive products. Petroglyphs, obelisk inscriptions and sarcophagi images all confirm that honeybees were considered sacred. Egyptian papyri refers to Bee Pollen as life-giving dust and frequently outlines how to use it as a sacred offering to the gods.

Written accounts tell of Roman legions who carried dried cakes of Bee Pollen for sustenance. Ancient Romans even made Virgil the official poet laureate of the honeybee, and Pliny refers to pollen when he writes, ". . . which the bee collect from the sweet juices of flowers, so beneficial to health."

Hippocrates recommended Bee Pollen as medicine for several ailments, and the Hindus taught that eating honey and pollen could produce health, vigor, happiness and wisdom. Orientals routinely used honey and pollen for medicinal purposes. Ancient Greeks referred to honey and pollen as the food of kings, believing that it would give them youth and vitality.

Anglo-Saxons also looked as Bee Pollen as a dietary staple. Both Welsh and Celtic myths are replete with numerous references to honey and pollen. These people drank a combination of wine, honey and pollen, believing it to be a life-sustaining elixir.

In the centuries which followed, men such as Emperor Charlemagne recorded that his subjects used pollen and honey on a daily basis. To illustrate how valuable these products were to Charlemagne, he required his people to take an annual inventory of their honey and pollen supplies. Taxes in the form of honey and pollen were routinely paid and gifts of honey or pollen were highly revered.

Almost every recorded religious or historical record praises honeybee products such as Bee Pollen. The Bible, Talmud, Torah, Koran, Russian and Slavic writings, and the Code of Islam refer to the beneficial healing and nutritive properties of Bee Pollen. On this continent, Aztec and Mayans worshiped the honeybee as evidenced by numerous images of honeycombs and pollen. Early American settlers became actively involved in honey production for table use.

Most modern day scientific investigation into Bee Pollen has taken place in Europe. Unfortunately, American scientists have shown minimal interest in European documentation, which supports the therapeutic value of Bee Pollen. Other researchers have already discovered that this remarkable food contains concentrations of almost every known nutrient. Reports from various areas of Europe and Russia confirm the fact that this remarkable substance has infinite value for health maintenance and disease treatment.

A NUTRIENT BREAKDOWN OF BEE POLLEN

VITAMIN AND MINERAL CONTENT: Bee Pollen is rich is B-vitamins including B-1, B-2, B-3 (Niacinamide), B-5 (Pantothenic Acid), B-6, and B-12. It also contains Vitamin C, A, E, Carotenoids, and Folic Acid. Approximately 20 percent of Bee Pollen is composed of amino acids and proteins. Bee Pollen is also extremely rich in rutin (17 percent), and has an undetermined amount of HGH (Human Growth Hormone) factor and Gonadatropin. Minerals found in Bee Pollen include: Magnesium, Calcium, Copper, Iron, Silica, Phosphorus, Sulfur, Chlorine, and Manganese. Essential fatty acids are also found in Bee Pollen.

CHARACTER: antibiotic, astringent, relaxant, tonic, nutritive

BODY SYSTEMS TARGETED: All body systems benefit from Bee Pollen with special emphasis on the reproductive, immune and nervous systems.

FORMS: Bee pollen can be purchased as a fresh powder, granules, canned, capsulized or in tablet form. Chewable wafers are particularly convenient and easy to take. A number of other specific nutritive supplements and herbs can be added to Bee Pollen to significantly potentiate its energy generating capacity. Botanicals like Gotu Kola, Ginseng, and Schizandra very nicely complement Bee Pollen. In addition, taking Bee Pollen with Royal Jelly or Propolis further enhances its biochemical properties.

Bee Pollen can be purchased in fresh granules, which usually come in sealed plastic bags. Canned Bee Pollen is best if it has been nitrogen packed. Bee Pollen tablets and capsulized Bee Pollen are the most convenient form of the substance and should be a varying shades of gold.

NOTE: In order to keep raw Bee Pollen fresh, after it has been opened, it should be refrigerated.

REGULATORY STATUS: Bee Pollen has no restrictions and is considered a food rather than an herb or vitamin.

SAFETY: If you suffer from pollen allergies, you should use Bee Pollen with caution. Ideally, the pollen should be harvested from local bees and should be initially taken in very small amounts. Start with a very small granule and work up to larger dose. If you experience itching in the throat, discontinue using it.

If no allergic symptoms result from taking tiny amounts of Bee Pollen, its dosage can be gradually increased over the period of a month. Frequently, allergic reactions to Bee Pollen are due to poor quality pollen or improperly cleaned supplies. Anyone who suffers from gout should avoid Bee Pollen in than it may elevate purine levels.

What Does Bee Pollen Do Best?

Modern science has discovered that Bee Pollen contains various properties which can speed healing, revitalize the body and even help protect cells against free radical damage. It has been successfully used to treat everything from prostate disorders to obesity.

Bee Pollen: Miracle Food?

It is important to know that bees recognize and select pollens which are rich in nitrogenous matter (amino acids) and leave poor quality pollens behind. As a food for human consumption, Bee Pollen is unsurpassed. Not only does it contain a complete complement of nutrients, its glucoside content helps to transport these nutrients into the bloodstream for use.

The Royal Society of Naturalists of Belgium and France have described Bee Pollen as a complete food which is rare and precious in its nutritive compounds.[24] Scientific studies have found that a person can live indefinitely on a diet consisting of Bee Pollen and water alone. A chemical analysis of Bee Pollen reveals that it contains every nutrient required to sustain life in addition to substances added by the bees. Research from the Royal Society of Naturalists has stated:

"The nutritional tests supervised by the station at Bures on hundreds of mice have demonstrated that pollen is a complete food, that it is possible to let several generations be born and live without the least sign if distress while nourishing them exclusively on pollen."[25]

The marvelous thing about Bee Pollen is the it contains virtually all the essential nutrients which are necessary to sustain life. Consequently, it is viewed by some as the perfect food complement to any diet, especially those that may be nutritionally unbalanced or deficient. Unfortunately, we routinely consume foods that have been artificially split or chemically manipulated which can destroy the benefits of the whole, natural food.

While our country may be considered prosperous and food supplies abound, nutrient-poor diets are becoming the rule rather than the exception. Bizarre cravings and the availability of "empty calorie" foods reflect the fact that many of us suffer from nutritional deficiencies and obesity. Bee Pollen helps to correct our body chemistry and to satisfy our nutrient needs.

Only Honey Bees Hold the Patent on Bee Pollen

Bee Pollen cannot be reproduced in the laboratory. Its chemical make-up is so complex that synthesizing it artificially has eluded even the best of our modern day technology. Some of the chemical compounds contained in Bee Pollen cannot even be correctly identified by scientists. In addition, what makes Bee Pollen so impressive is that it contains many nutrients that animal products do not have.

Clearly, Bee Pollen is one of nature's most complete foods. It is so impressive in its nutrient array, that some experts believe it could be the answer to world hunger. In this regard, increased harvesting of the pollen would be necessary. This abundant, natural resource has remained relatively untapped and may offer a valuable protein food for people plagued by famine or economic decline. To summarize, Bee Pollen is rich in protein, free amino acids, an impressive vitamin array and folic acid which cannot be artificially duplicated.

Chemical Composition of Bee Pollen (per 100 parts)

AMINO ACIDS

arginine	4.7 parts
Histidine	1.5 parts
isoleucine	4.7 parts
leucine	5.6 parts

methionine	1.7 parts
phenylalanine	3.5 parts
threonine	4.6 parts
tryptophan	1.6 parts
valine	6.0 parts
glutamic acid	9.1 parts

VITAMINS (per 1,000 milligrams of Bee Pollen)

Thiamine (vitamin B-1)	9.2 mg
Riboflavin (vitamin B-3)	18.50 mg
Niacinamide (vitamin B-3)	200 mg
Pyridoxine (vitamin B-6)	5 mg
Pantothenic acid (vitamin B-5)	30-50 mg
Folic acid	3.64-6.8 mg
Lactoflavin	
Vitamin A (carotenoids)	.5-.9 mg
Vitamin C	7-15 mg
Vitamin E	Trace

B12 see p. 21 (handwritten margin note)

MINERALS (per 1,000 milligrams of Bee Pollen)

Potassium	600 mg

OTHER MINERALS

magnesium	1%-12%
calcium	1%-15%
copper	.05%-.08%
iron	.01%-.30%
silica	2%-10%
phosphorus	1%-20%
sulfur	1%
chlorine	1%
manganese	1.4%

Bee Pollen also contains 17 percent of rutin (vitamin P).

HORMONES

• Gonadotropic and Estrogenic
• HGH (human growth hormone factor)

Bee Pollen and Rutin

According to scientists at the Institute of Apiculture in Taranov, Russia: "Honeybee pollen is the riches source of vitamins found in Nature in a single food. Even if Bee Pollen had none of its other vital ingredients, its content of rutin alone would justify taking at least a teaspoon daily, if for no other reason than strengthening the capillaries. Pollen is extremely rich in rutin and may have the highest content of any source. . ."[26]

Rutin is a glucoside which helps to increase the strength and integrity of blood cell walls. The rutin content of pollen also helps minimize bleeding and encourage coagulation. Consequently, for those who bruise easily, rutin is extremely beneficial. Rutin also helps to strengthen the heart and control high blood pressure by helping to regulate blood flow.

Amino Acids, Protein and Bee Pollen

Incredibly, Bee Pollen is actually richer in proteins than any animal source available. It contains more amino acids than beef, eggs or cheese of an equivalent weight. The fact that Bee Pollen contains such high concentrations of nutrients like protein in such tiny amounts is quite amazing, to say the least. It's not hard to see why it serves as such a superior source of energy and anabolic regeneration.

Bee Pollen, Energy and Endurance:
A Panacea for Athletes

Many Olympic athletes have routinely used Bee Pollen to increase their stamina during training. Ancient Greek marathon runners recognized the value of Bee Pollen and used it to increase their endurance and strength.

Members of the Russian ice hockey team along with other Soviet athletes have traditionally used Bee Pollen to rejuvenate themselves and maintain their energy levels. Soviet scientists regard Bee Pollen as the most desirable food that mother nature has to offer. Finnish Olympic athletes routinely use Bee Pollen to supplement their diets taking dosages which vary from four to ten tablets daily depending on anticipated physical demands. Steve Reddick, a Gold Medalist on the U.S. Relay Team at the Montreal games in 1976, stated:

"It [Bee Pollen] gives me a lot more energy too. I used to take honey but this Bee Pollen is far better. I take three pills a day."[27]
Reddick set an unofficial world record for the 100 meter dash in 1975.

Many coaches of all kinds recommend Bee Pollen to their athletes. Some of these include Jack Gimmeler, track coach at St. Jon's University in Queens, John Moon, track coach at Seton Hall University, Doug Boyd, trainer at Fairleight Dickenson University and Tommy Smith, at Oberlin in Ohio.[28]

Coach Tom McNab, who has coached a number of British Athletes says:

"In October of 1973, I was asked to test the efficacy of a bee pollen product. I was initially skeptical of the results likely to be obtained by use of this product. However, I asked five athletes training under me to take bee pollen in accordance with the manufacturer's directions; that is, one to three pills a day. Within a period of 12 months, the athletic performance of all of the five athletes taking bee pollen had substantially improved."[29]

Underweight athletes seem to particularly benefit from Bee Pollen. A rise in body weight and lean muscle mass has been observed. Bee Pollen is particularly rich in B-complex vitamins, minerals like potassium and a variety of amino acids, the building blocks of proteins. These nutrients support the glandular system which is responsible for surges of vitality and increased stamina.

Energizing Botanicals that Enhance Bee Pollen

GOTU KOLA: Considered a restorative for the nervous system, this herb promotes energy, alertness and mental clarity.

SIBERIAN GINSENG: This herbal has been traditionally used in the Far East to treat exhaustion and debility. It also facilitates faster healing and can act to promote lower cholesterol levels.

PANAX GINSENG: Used in China for over 5,000 years, Panax Ginseng is an excellent tonic and natural stimulant for the immune system, providing stamina and endurance.

SCHIZANDRA: Considered an all around tonic, Schizandra acts to tone and strengthen body organs.

Beehive Food Complement Each Other

ROYAL JELLY: When combined with Bee Pollen, Royal Jelly works to normalize body systems, protect against infection by boosting the immune system and provides a superior array of vital nutrients required for optimal health.

Pollution, Poisons and Pollen

Radiation, chemical pollutants and a whole host of allergens constantly assault our immune systems, creating all kinds of havoc with our antibody responses, while bombarding our cells with dangerous free radicals. The Center for Disease Control and the Environmental Protection Agency have stated that over the course of one year, we will be exposed to over 200 different forms of radioactive toxins and over 60,000 individual chemical poisons.[30]

Most of us have become acquainted with the threat of free radicals, which enter our cellular systems with each and every breath of air we inhale. By now, we're all interested in supplementing our diet with antioxidants which can afford our tissues protection from the damage caused by free radical encounters.

Many of us are unaware that Bee Pollen is an excellent free radical scavenger that can effectively protect our bodies from the devastating side effects of pollutant or radiation exposure. Clinical documentation has supported the ability of Bee Pollen to counteract the effect these toxins have on human health.[31]

"Bee Pollen significantly reduced the usual side effects of both radium and cobalt-60 radiotherapy in twenty-five women who had been treated for inoperable uterine cancer."[32]

For these women, taking Bee Pollen resulted in less nausea, stronger immune system responses, and an increase in red and white blood cells. In addition, unlike the typical response to radiation treatments, these patients sustained a good appetite and avoided the expected sleep disruption and standard weakness that usually accompany such therapy. These women took approximately 20 grams of Bee Pollen, about two teaspoons, three time daily.   2 T

Allergies and Bee Pollen

Developing an actual "immunity" against allergies is exactly what many experts believe Bee Pollen can accomplish. When we encounter an allergen, our immune system produces produces more histamine which causes an inflammatory response, (ie: itchy, watery eyes, red, swollen nose, etc.). Laboratory tests have found that taking Bee Pollen can inhibit this response, thereby decreasing the miserable symptoms which usually accompany an allergic reaction. Quercitin, a bioflavonoid, is in Bee Pollen and significantly inhibits the production and release of histamine. Clearly it contributes to the ability of Bee Pollen to decrease allergic responses.

NOTE: Bee Pollen should not be confused with the type of pollen carried by the wind in the Spring. It is this wind-born pollen (anemophiles) which can cause terrific allergic responses in some people. Bee Pollen is much heavier and tackier than this other form of pollen. It is collected from the legs of honeybees by special devices which are placed in hive entry ways. While it may cause an allergic reaction in some individuals, allergy symptoms which originate from Bee Pollen are relatively rare.[33]

Many individuals who suffer from pollen allergies and hay fever can safely take Bee Pollen. Consider the following data:

*73 percent of patients with hay fever averaged a 75 percent improvement when given Bee Pollen orally.

*78 percent of asthma patients averaged a 75 percent improvement after taking Bee Pollen.

*17.8 percent of hay fever sufferers and 33.3 percent of asthmatics experienced a complete improvement on oral Bee Pollen supplements.[34]

The earlier Bee Pollen supplementation was begun prior to allergy season, the greater rate of its success.

Weight Control and Bee Pollen

Bee Pollen is rich in lecithin which helps to breakdown fats. Its primary role in weight control appears to be its ability to stabilize a faulty metabolism. In addition, Bee Pollen can help to balance body chemistry by providing a total array of nutrients. By so doing, abnormal food cravings or unusually stimulated appetites can be controlled.

Generally speaking, if weight loss is desired, Bee Pollen should be taken alone on an empty stomach. The reasoning behind this is based on the fact that Bee Pollen sugars are rapidly metabolized and in the process boost the rate of calorie burning or thermogenesis.

Bee Pollen and Digestion

Bee Pollen contains an inverted sugar which does not ferment in the intestinal tract. In addition, it has a soothing effect on any intestinal inflammation and is considered a natural lubricant. This lubricating action in combination with its natural fatty acid content promote peristalsis, which helps to prevent constipation and gas.

NOTE: Taking large dosages of Bee Pollen can result in some minor gastrointestinal irritation or a laxative effect.

The Natural Antibiotic Content of Bee Pollen

Bee Pollen contains differing quantities of a particular antibiotic which fights E. coli and Proteus organisms which can cause serious diseases. The antibiotic action of Bee Pollen was found to be effective against salmonella and other strains of colibacillus.[35]

Experts that have studied Bee Pollen believe it can act as a potent bactericide. Apparently, bacteria cannot exist in Bee Pollen. In addition, taking Bee Pollen regularly is believed to increase the body's resistance to infection.

Several laboratory tests have found that a particular compound in the pollen inhibits the growth of several types of harmful bacteria.

Bee Pollen and Cancer

A report in the *Journal of the National Cancer Institute* of October 1948 stated that Bee Pollen was given to laboratory test animals which had been bred to develop tumors. They found that certain amounts of Bee Pollen appeared to either prevent or inhibit the growth of malignant cells. An additional report from the Department of Agriculture stated:

"In some preliminary experiments, it was observed that the addition of pollen to the food of mice of the C3H strain (a form of cancer) delayed the appearance of spontaneous mammary (breast) tumors eight to ten weeks."[36]

Laboratory tests have strongly suggested that adding Bee Pollen to food can act as a significant anti-carcinogenic component. Of interest is the fact that large amounts of Bee Pollen were not required to create this effect, a fact which supports the notion that nutrients found in Bee Pollen are highly concentrated and balanced.

Bee Pollen: Aging Retardant?

The anti-aging properties of Bee Pollen have been the focus of more attention as large numbers of baby boomers enter middle age and beyond. Over thirty years ago, Russian researchers endeavored to explain why a certain group of Russians had lived to be over 100 years old. The one factor these people all shared in common was that their primary food was honey. Subsequent observation concluded that it probably was not the honey alone that promoted such longevity, but the waste products from the beehive that were also consumed.[37] It was this residue which contained almost 100 percent pure pollen, which is thought to have endowed these centenarians with sustained health.

Additional research found that pollen-eating Russians enjoyed much longer sexual potency and fertility.[38]

Observations of older people who consistently use Bee Pollen strongly suggest that they enjoy better physical and mental health. Another component of Bee Pollen which stimulates the endocrine system and promotes rejuvenation is aspartic acid. In addition, the natural constituents of Bee Pollen contain estrogen and androgen which act as biological stimulants. These gonadotropins can stimulate a slow metabolism and enhance the regeneration of cells.

These cell sustaining hormones, naturally found in Bee Pollen, seem to act as a tonic to reinvigorate an aging system.

Dr. Paavo O. Airola in his book, Health Secrets from Europe says: "It has been suggested that Bulgarians Rumanians, Russians and other East European peoples known for their enviable record of longevity have to thank lactic acid for their excellent health and youthful vitality. Probably the most beneficial effect of pollen is that taken internally, it quickly produces the same anti-putrefactive effects as lactic acid foods, and thus contributes to a healthy digestive system and good assimilation of nutrients . . . absolute prerequisites for good health and long life"

Some studies have suggested that taking pollen can reverse the aging process seen in skin that lacks elasticity. For this reason, in some countries, Bee Pollen is used as an anti-aging cosmetic for the firming and restoring of skin tone.

Interestingly, the use of HGH (Human Growth Hormone) has recently made front page headlines as one of the most promising anti-aging compounds found. One of the first indications that aging is in reversal is a restoration of skin tone. Bee Pollen contains unmeasured amounts of HGH factor.

The HGH (Human Growth Hormone) Factor in Bee Pollen

Mice that have been given Bee Pollen in combination with other dietary nutrients have exhibited an acceleration of growth. While this result has been attributed to the notion that the pollen modifies the metabolism of carbohydrates, the HGH (Human Growth Hormone) factor may play a role here. Recently, the profound value of HGH in slowing and even reversing the aging process has made front page news.

TRADITIONAL USES OF BEE POLLEN

*Indians in South American used a combination of honey and pollen to treat burns and other skin injuries. Today Europeans still use honey, pollen and cod liver oil to promote healing.

*Bee Pollen mixed with honey and warm milk has traditionally been used for sore throats and laryngitis.

*Poultices made up honey and pollen have been used in Europe for generations to treat respiratory ailments including bronchitis and asthma.

*An Oriental anti-aging formula included Bee Pollen, Honey, Ginseng and Orange Peel.

PRIMARY APPLICATIONS OF BEE POLLEN

- Allergies
- Anemia
- Antibiotic
- Appetite (can act as a stimulant or suppressant depending on need)
- Asthma
- Blood builder
- Capillary weakness
- Chronic fatigue
- Immune system booster
  Impotence
  Infertility
- Kidney disorders
- Longevity
- Menopausal symptoms
  Prostate diseases
- Ulcers

NOTE: Some people stand by Bee Pollen as an effective treatment for diseases like Multiple Sclerosis.

Chapter 3

PROPOLIS: MOTHER NATURE'S INFEC-
TION FIGHTER AND HEALER

Propolis is another marvelous nutrient made by honey bees. Used for millennia, it has the ability to provide protection against infectious invaders, promote healing and regeneration of tissue, and provide a superior source of energy and endurance. Clearly, it is one of nature's most versatile substances and is considered a breakthrough supplement in the world of natural therapies. The intrinsic value of Propolis is being rediscovered not only by athletes, who want maximum health and performance, but by health conscious people everywhere.

What Is Bee Propolis?

Propolis is a resinous substance which is gathered by honeybees from deciduous tree bark and leaves. It is a sticky material that bees very efficiently use to seal hive holes or cracks. This natural "glue" is cleverly utilized by the industrious honeybee to provide exterior protection to the hive against the invasion of any outside contaminants. Bees purposefully place this tacky substance in the area which leads into the beehive, not only to prevent the entrance of intruders, but to sterilize bees brushing up against it from infection. Before it is used in the hive, honeybees take this sap, combine it with nectar found in their own secretions, and eventually end up with a mixture consisting of wax, pollen and bee bread. For this reason, just chewing on a wad of tree resin won't produce the same therapeutic results as Propolis. Bees must transform the resin into Propolis, and only they know how.

Bee Propolis: Ancient Healer

Propolis has existed for at least 45 million years, and like Royal Jelly and Bee Pollen, it is experiencing a rediscovery in the late twentieth century. It is an excellent natural antibiotic and immune system booster and in the animal kingdom, creates one of the most sterile environments known.

Propolis has traditionally been used to treat a whole host of ailments. Hippocrates prescribed the material to promote the healing of sores and ulcers, both internal and external.[39] Several mythical legends refer to the magical activities of bees that resulted in the production of what was thought to be a miracle substance. In A.D. 23-79, Pliny, a Roman scholar recorded, "current physicians use Propolis as a medicine because it extracts stings and all substances embedded in the flesh, reduced swelling, softens indurations, soothes pains of the sinews, and heals sores when it appears hopeless for them to mend."[40]

In later centuries, several herbal registries referred to Propolis as a clammy substance that can provide extraordinary healing. *Culpepper's Complete Herbal* refers to ointments made with Propolis as good for inflammations and fever. Over and over again, cultures all over the world have recognized the ability of Propolis to fight infection, to promote healing and to support immune function.

"Propolis has been known since ancient times . . . It was used in the Soviet Union during World War II for the treatment of tenacious battle wounds. For many years, Propolis has been a popular medicine in numerous countries in Eastern and Western Europe. Because of its extensive use, it has attracted great interest in medicine."[41]

The widespread use of Propolis in the Soviet Union for infection earned it the appropriate title of "Russian Penicillin." Clearly, Propolis is regarded as the strongest and most powerful natural antibiotic. Today, clinical studies continue to unravel its mysteries and applications. Like other beehive foods, Propolis is most definitely for people.

Active Compounds

Dr. K. Lund Aagaard who is considered a well qualified authority on Propolis has said, "Nineteen substances of different chemical structure have been identified so far."[42] These compounds include a number of substances which belong to the flavonoid family including betulene and isovanillin.

Vitamin and Mineral Content

According to researchers at the Second Leningrad Scientific Conference on the Application of Apiculture (bee culture) in Medicine, Bee Propolis is rich in:

Vitamin A (carotene)
Vitamin B1
Vitamin B2
Vitamin B3
biotin
an array of bioflavonoids
albumin
calcium
magnesium
iron
zinc
silica
potassium
phosphorus
manganese
cobalt
copper

NOTE: Propolis contains 500 more bioflavonoids (vitamin P) than is found in oranges.

Except for vitamin K, Propolis has all the known vitamins. Of the fourteen minerals required by the body, Propolis contains them all with the exception of sulfur.

Propolis is comprised of 50 percent to 70 percent resins and balsams, 30 percent to 50 percent wax, 5 percent to 10 percent Bee Pollen and 10 percent essential oils.[43]

Like Royal Jelly and Bee Pollen, Propolis also contains a number of unidentified compounds which work together synergistically to create a perfectly balanced, nutritive substance.

Amino Acids

Sixteen amino acids have been identified in propolis.

CHARACTER: antibacterial, antiviral, antibiotic, antifungal, anti-inflammatory, antioxidant

FORMS: Lozenges, Capsules, Salve, Tablets, Granules, Powder

The capsulized form of Propolis is convenient and more easily ingested that loose powders or granules. Capsulized Propolis contains a concentrated dry extract of the substance that is easy to take.

NOTE: While it is not necessary, it is always preferable to store Propolis in a cool place.

Propolis: A Superior Source of Bioflavonoids

Bioflavonoids may sound like a mouthful to pronounce. They are nothing less that remarkable in their anti-inflammatory action and are sometimes referred to as vitamin P. As a therapeutic substance, Propolis owes much to its rich bioflavonoid content. Recent research is just beginning to uncover the effectiveness of bioflavonoids in healing broken capillaries (bruising), mending blood vessels, and inhibiting the production and release of histamine.

"Over 500 scientific papers on bioflavonoids have been published in reputable medical journals around the world. Clinical reports have shown that bioflavonoid therapy is effective in such diversified conditions as rheumatic fever, spontaneous abortions and miscarriages, high blood pressure, respiratory infections, hemorrhoids, cirrhosis of the liver, etc."[44]

In light of the extraordinary value of bioflavonoids, Propolis stands out as a potent and superior source. It is the flavonoid content of Propolis which enables it to fight infection and inhibit inflammation.

"The protein coating around the virus in maintained by the flavonoids in propolis; these flavonoids keep the virus inactive. It is the same as being immune to the virus, but only with the presence of bioflavonoids as in the Propolis."[45]

Propolis: Nature's Penicillin and Infection Protectant

Finding a natural antibiotic with none of the side effects of synthetic drug varieties would unquestionably be considered a remarkable discovery. Propolis is just such a substance. In Poland, scientists used 56 different strains of staphylococcus to test Propolis and conclude:

"All strains whose sensitivity to Propolis was certain were highly resistant to the tested antibiotics."[46]

What this means is than Propolis was able to fight bacterial strains which had become resistant to man-made antibiotic drugs. A 1992 clinical study further revealed:

"Propolis, a honeybee hive product is thought to exhibit a broad spectrum of activities including antibiotic, antiviral, anti-inflammatory and tumor growth inhibition."[47]

NOTE: The bee is the only insect to have been found free of bacteria due to the antibiotic action of Propolis.[48]

The Disatrous Consequences of Over-prescribing Antibiotics

It's no secret that medical and scientific communities are alarmed at what seems like an inevitable calamity. Because antibiotics have been routinely and very casually prescribed for everything from a hangnail to a slight cough, bacterial strains are mutating so as to eventually render these drugs useless. In other words, the bugs are outwitting the drugs. The fear lies in the inevitable inability to design another stronger, wider spectrum antibiotic variation, thereby disabling our ability to stay "one step ahead" of new bacterial strains. In addition, antibiotic drugs disable our immune systems and make us all the more susceptible to future infection.

A Natural, No Side-Effect Antibiotic

Propolis has been used for centuries to treat infections without the drawbacks of synthetic pharmaceuticals. It has demonstrated its ability to fight infections of every kind while boosting the action of the human immune system; something that synthetic antibiotics are not able to do. A number of clinical studies have supported the ability of Propolis to fight microbial invaders of all kinds.[49]

Viral Infections and Propolis

We all know how hard it is to kill or even disable a virus. Propolis exerts a number of multi-faceted effects on viruses. One of these actions in quite unique. Propolis does something altogether different to impair viruses thereby inhibiting their reproduction and infectious potential. Consider the following quote:

"Bioflavonoids in Propolis have a protective effect on virus infections. Let me explain. Viruses are enclosed in a protein coat. As long as it remains unbroken, the infectious and dangerous material remains imprisoned and is harmless to the organism. We have found that an enzyme which normally removes the protein coat is being inhibited; thus, dangerous viral material is kept locked in."[50]

"Under the influence of Propolis, the virus-fighting power of phagocytosis is strengthened. The content of the protective virus-fighting protein, properdin, starts to rise in the blood. There is a speeding of the detoxification power of certain antibodies."[51]

Bacterial Infections:

The ability of Propolis to combat bacterial infection has also been documented in Russia where it has been extensively tested. Test results concluded that: "Bee Propolis. . .has such self-activating power, it sustains its antibacterial characteristics even if stored for many years under proper conditions."[52]

SORE THROATS: Taking propolis in lozenge or other liquid form can be used directly on the tissues of a sore throat. Using capsules or tablets is also recommended. Opening up capsules of Propolis and making a Propolis gargle has also been effective. A sore throat, even if caused by a viral infection, would greatly benefit from Propolis therapy. Sore throats are caused from an inflammation and infection of the mucous membranes of the throat.

HERPES ZOSTER: Herpes is caused by a viral infection that creates

Shingles

painful skin eruptions. Dr. Franz Feiks found that using a five percent solution of Propolis once a day had an impressive curative effect on Herpes. "In all of the twenty cases I treated, pain disappeared within forty-eight hours and did not reappear. In three cases, only itching persisted over a long period of time."[53]

FLU: Scientists in Russia have found that Propolis has significant flu-inhibiting actions. As we know, influenza is caused by a virus that is extremely hard to treat and resistant to drug therapy. Russian research has conclusively discovered that using Propolis was found to, "boost a preventative benefit not only for the flu but other virus disease."[54]

Propolis Potentiating Effect of Synthetic Drugs

If it's necessary to take synthetic antibiotic drugs for a particular infection, supplementing that drug with Propolis can boost its effectiveness. Russian research discovered that:

"It was shown that Propolis combined with antibiotics (tetracycline, monomycin, levomycetin) intensifies and prolongs the antimicrobial action... results show that using Propolis in combination with antibiotics results in an increase in the therapeutical efficiency of the antibiotics."[55]

Propolis Anti-Inflammatory Properties

As mentioned earlier, the rich bioflavonoid content of Propolis makes an excellent natural anti-inflammatory. The use of anti-inflammatory drugs today is unprecedented. Ibuprofen, Naprosyn, and myriads of prescription and over-the counter pain killers and antihistamines are taken in tremendous amounts to combat symptoms of inflammation. The inflammatory response can be initiated by conditions like arthritis, rheumatism, allergies and infections of every kind. Redness, swelling, pain, fever and the release of histamine causing watery eyes, runny nose and sneezing are all part of body "inflammations." Because bioflavonoids have the ability to inhibit the uncontrolled release of histamine, the miserable symptoms that accompany inflammation can be reduced.

Allergies

Technically, Propolis can be considered a source of histamine and serotonin, two desirable substances under normal circumstances. It is when histamine leaks from mast cells that we experience histamine induced symptoms, which are not desirable. Exposure to certain allergens such as dust, pollen molds etc. can initiate this mast cell leakage which can lead to sneezing, hives, itchy, watery eyes, sinus back drip etc. Blocking this mast cell leakage can significantly reduce miserable allergic symptoms. This is precisely what Propolis can accomplish.

"We have found that this can be done with the use of the bioflavonoids in Propolis. They can block the acids that would break into the cells and cause the release of the allergy-causing substances. Again, we see that Propolis can create this form of built-in immunity."[56]

Propolis: Powerful Healing Agent

Propolis has a marvelous toning and healing effect on epithelial tissue, which comprises the outer layer of our skin, mucous and serous membranes, and lines our organs, glands and cavities from the inside of our mouths to our gastrointestinal tract.

"Considered your first line of defense, epithelial tissue is involved in all infections, inflammations, and immunological problems due to internal or external harmful agents. It serves the general functions of enclosing and protecting, producing secretions and excretions, and acting to absorb nutrients. It also has specialized functions such as movement of substances through ducts, production of cells and reception of stimuli."[57]

Even when skin tissue was damaged by radiation, which is considered the single most destructive stressor to the body, using alcohol based solutions of Propolis therapeutically resulted in increased healing. For this reason, using Propolis for ulcers and skin disorders is highly recommended.

After observing the effects of Propolis on over 50,000 people in Scandinavia, consider what Dr. K. Lund Aagaard has to say about the healing properties of Propolis:

"The field of influence of Propolis is extremely broad. It includes cancer, infection of the urinary tract, swelling of the throat, gout, open wounds, sinus congestion, colds, influenza, bronchitis, gastritis, diseases, of the ears, periodontal disease, intestinal infections, ulcers, eczema eruptions, pneumonia, arthritis, lung disease, stomach virus, headaches, Parkinson's disease, bile infections, sclerosis, circulation deficiencies, warts, conjunctivitis and hoarseness.

"Propolis helps regulate hormones and is an antibiotic substance that stimulates the natural resistance of the body. . .Propolis is also efficient against conditions caused by bacteria, viruses or different fungi. Propolis cures many diseases because it is a special substance with strong effect."[58]

ULCERS: Concerning the ability of Propolis to treat gastrointestinal ulcers and other disorders, clinicians reported:

"On the basis of the facts cited from literature, we can draw the conclusion that Bee Propolis is a medicinal preparation with bacteriocidal, antitoxic, anti-inflammatory and anesthetizing properties. In addition, it normalizes the secreting function of the stomach. It can be recommended for the treatment of patients who are suffering from ulcers (abscesses) in the stomach and/or duodenum. Recover occurs more quickly with treatment by Propolis than it does with the use of common medicines."[59]

SKIN AILMENTS: Because Propolis can stimulate cell regeneration while it reduces inflammation, it is ideal as a therapeutic agent for a variety of skin disorders including, acne, pimples, eczema, burns, abrasions, and wounds. Propolis has been routinely used in salve form by burn units in Russia.

"Scientist Dr. G.F. Zablina tells that Propolis is able to curb inflammation and disinfect wounds. In addition, it is able to stimulate new skin growth. Dr. Zablina recommends its use to heal infected burns."[60]

NATURAL ANESTHETIC: James Devlin, Ph.D. a great advocate of Propolis has written, "As I can testify, the anesthetic and pain relieving effects of Propolis cream are really quite marvelous. . .Even the ancients knew that Propolis works wonders on damaged skin."[61]

Propolis and Cancer

In 1991, the Comprehensive Cancer Center and Institute of Cancer Research of Columbia University initiated a study on Propolis and its cancer fighting potential. The caffeic acid phenethyl ester (CAPE) contained in Propolis was found to have an anti-viral action as well as an inhibitory action on certain types of cancer. Continuing research on the possible use of this caffeic acid for cancer is on-going at Columbia University.[62] Their documented research reveals that CAPE was a valuable therapeutic agent against a certain adenovirus and a form of mammary based tumor virus.[63] Romanian studies have shown that cancer patients treated with Propolis went into remission.[64] Regarding Propolis, Columbia University research concluded:

"The invention [Propolis] provides a method for substantially inhibiting the growth of transformed cells without substantially inhibiting the growth of normal cells. . .The transformed cells may comprise carcinoma or melanoma cells. In the preferred embodiments, the subject is a human and the transformed cells are human carcinoma or melanoma cells, such as human breast carcinoma cells, colon carcinoma cells, renal carcinoma cells, or melanoma cells."[65]

Another more recent study on CAPE concluded:

"Previous work from this laboratory established that caffeic acid esters, present in the Propolis of honeybee hives, are potent inhibitors of human colon tumor cell growth, suggesting that these compounds may possess antitumor activity against colon carcinogenesis."[66]

It is the CAPE found in Propolis which is responsible for its cancer fighting potential. As the quote indicates, this acid can stop the proliferation of mutated cells (cancerous) while leaving normal cells undamaged. Most of us are aware of the devastating effects chemotherapy and radiation treatments have on normal tissue. These methods of cancer treatment are not selective and are just as toxic to healthy cells. For this reason, Propolis, as well as other beehive products should be taken to treat disease, not only for their ability to target diseased tissue, but for their immunostimulatory action as well. Their benefits are two-fold.

Propolis: A Complete and Live Food for Raw Energy

While Propolis has exhibited a variety of very impressive therapeutic actions, its ability to energize the body and restore vigor and stamina is an added bonus. It is the ability of Propolis to stimulate the thymus gland which is thought to result in its energizing properties. John Diamond, a medical doctor and President of the International Academy of Preventative Medicine has related:

"Of all the natural supplements I have tested, the one that seems to be the most strengthening to the thymus, and hence the life energy, is Bee Resin, or Bee Propolis, a resin secreted by trees and then metabolized by the bees . . . Our life energy is the source of our physical and mental well-being, of glowing health, of the joy of living. . .unfortunately 95 percent of the general population tests low on the life energy scale."

Dr. Diamond strongly believes that an underactive thymus gland is responsible for weakness and fatigue in many individuals. Hence, using Propolis to stimulate the thymus has a dual benefit in that it invigorates the body and fortifies its ability to resist disease.

Propolis: A Preventative Supplement

"Propolis may be used by everyone, sick or healthy, as a means of protection against microorganisms."[67] Today, the key to good health is prevention rather than after-the-fact treatment. While most of us will inevitably experience sickness or injury, we should be striving to protect and boost our immune systems to fight off the many contaminants we are exposed to daily. Because new, stronger and less treatable viruses and bacterial infections are evolving, taking Propolis is more important today than ever before. The widespread over-prescription of synthetic antibiotic drugs may leave us facing a future epidemic which some scientists have referred to as the coming "modern day black plague." Our only option is to fortify ourselves against such infections. Propolis has an impressive track record for doing just that and should be taken as a complementary supplement to a good nutritious diet.

Dr. Roy Kupsinel, a medical physician has stated:

"I prescribe Propolis for many of my patients as a safe nutritional supplement. When taken regularly, it actually creates an antibiotic disease-fighting reaction to almost any illness. . .without dangerous side effects. The bees have relied upon Propolis for 46 million years. They must be doing something right because beehives contain less bacteria and are more sterile than hospitals! Propolis is incredible."[68]

James Devlin, Ph.D. writes: ". . . consider the preventative powers of Propolis. People who take propolis regularly, and I'm one of them, simple never get sick. The most common remark is 'and I haven't had a cold or the flu or a sinus infection since I've been on the stuff.'"

NOTE: Honeybees use Propolis to protect the hive from contamination. It can exert the same effect on human physiology, helping to protect us from the threat of microorganism invasion.

PRIMARY APPLICATIONS OF PROPOLIS

- allergies
  bruises
  burns
  cancer
  herpes zoster
- fatigue
  sore throats
  nasal congestion
- respiratory ailments
  acne
  skin disorders
  sunburn
  shingles
  respiratory infections
  flu
  colds
  coughs
- ulcers
  wounds

It is vital to remember that Propolis is considered a marvelous and important medicine in Western and Eastern Europe. Its extensive use and versatility make it one of nature's most valuable therapeutic foods.

". . . it (Propolis) is used today in almost all branches of medicine . . . internal medicine, otolaryngology, dermatology, gynecology . . . as a blood coagulating agent, in various wounds, purulent processes, burns, and so on. It is very often used with the other hive products to invigorate the patient after physical or mental fatigue and exhaustion."[69]

Chapter 4

HONEY: NUTRITIOUS NECTAR-FILLED CULINARY DELIGHT

Bees make honey from the nectar they sip from flower blossoms. A long and tedious process is required to transform nectar into the thick, golden substance we call honey. Like each product produced by the honeybee, painstaking care and a number of intricate steps are essential to create this beehive food. Honey is no exception. This sweet, nutritious edible "gold" is a viscous fluid which is exclusively created by the honeybee. To date, even the most sophisticated modern techniques have failed to synthetically manufacture Honey. Like Royal Jelly, Propolis and Bee Pollen, Honey is only available from Mother Nature's storehouse of nutritive foods. It is a precious and often coveted substance that has fascinated and pleased cultures from the dawn of time.

Honey's History: A Sweet Story

The ancient Greeks called it one of nature's most precious gifts; the Assyrians, Chinese and Romans routinely prescribed it for its medicinal value; numerous Biblical references refer to the "Honeycomb" the "Land of Milk and Honey" and the Enlightenment" which comes from eating Honey. Hippocrates, considered the Father of Medicine, recorded, "Honey drink cures phlegm and calms down cough." He was one of the first known advocates of using Honey and Vinegar for fevers and other ailments. Virgil, one of the most famous of Roman poets wrote, "Next, I sing of Honey, the heavenly ethereal gift. . .sweet scented Honey, fragrant with thyme.

All of these ancient cultures believed that the daily use of Honey would insure health and longevity. All kinds of wines and foods were routinely mixed with honey, which was viewed by all peoples as a "treasure which the gods provided for your health."[70]

Avicenna, an Arabian physician referred to a number of Honey-based remedies in his Canon: "Honey helps when you have a runny nose, cheers you up, makes you feel fit, facilitates digestion, gets rid of wind, improves appetite."[71] Of all the ancient cultures, it was the Egyptians who prized Honey enough to use it as a form of money. In addition, numerous Egyptian scenes depict beekeeping in which multiple hives were cared for and harvested. Honey cakes, Honeycombs and jars of Honey are also referred to. Clearly, the honeybee was venerated for its life-giving foods. Hieroglyphics refer to Honey as the "universal healer," and jars of honey were routinely placed in the tombs of the dead. Due to its superior preservative properties, Honey was an integral part of the formula used for mummification of the body. The symbol of the honeybee as it relates to deity within Pharaoh's reign is commonly found on papyri, tomb walls and on artifacts. The artistic use of the Honeybee to evoke notions of life and preservation attests to its intrinsic value as a food and therapeutic agent.

Throughout history, Honey has been used to treat open wounds and to fight infection. Unfortunately, with the advent of refined sugar, Honey took a back seat to other more popular sweeteners. Today, it is experiencing a resurgence as an often overlooked beehive food that is full of nutritive and medicinal value.

How Honey Is Made

When a forager bee alights on a flower, it sucks a tiny amount of nectar through what is called a proboscis to a honey sac. It is within this sac that the transformation of nectar to honey begins. There the nectar is mixed with acid secretions to eventually form the Honey. Substantial amounts of nectar are required to produce significant amounts of Honey. Flying the a distance of some three miles may be necessary to obtain the amount of nectar needed to fill the sac. When the sac is full, the Honeybee returns to the hive, where a receiving bee takes the nectar and continues the process. Here, the nectar is changed, enriched and concentrated after which it is dropped into the empty cells of the honeycomb. To produce a single pound of Hone, bees must provide the hive with over 70,000 loads of nectar. An industrious beehive can produce up to 300 pounds of Honey per season.

Interestingly, the high water content of this nectar solution must be removed in order for the nectar to ripen into honey. To facilitate this very difficult task, worker bees continually transfer the nectar from one cell to another, allowing it to dry out. In time, the substance thickens to the point where it is placed within one cell. Because the forming honey is still too moist, large colonies of bees will band together, and by fanning their wings in unison, will complete the drying process.

Only after the Honey is deemed adequately thick and dry enough will the bees seal the filled comb with wax. Even at this point, the Honey is still considered "green" and will continue to ripen within the comb cell. Bees do such a marvelous job of sealing each cell that honey preserved in this way will keep for years. Honey can be eaten directly from the honeycomb. If the Honey is harvested for commercial purposes, it is simply strained and heated enough to liquefy so it can be poured and sealed in jars.

NOTE: A honeybee may have to travel as far as 40,000 miles to produce enough honey to fill a one-pound jar.

The Chemical Composition of Honey

Many people regard honey as simply another choice in a variety of "sweeteners" available. Honey is a highly nutritious beehive food that does much more than just merely sweeten. While the composition of Honey can vary depending on its sources, all types of raw Honey contain valuable nutrients. Raw, unprocessed Honey is the most nutritious type, and is best for its therapeutic value as a medicinal agent.

Over 75 individual substances are found in honey. Glucose and fructose are the major sugars found in honey and are monosaccharides (simple sugars). Simple sugars are more easily assimilated that other forms and don't require the additional processing necessary for white sugar, a disaccharide, to be digested. Honey is an invert sugar composed of 38 percent fructose, 31 percent glucose, 1 percent sucrose and 9 percent additional sugars.

Honey contains proteins, carbohydrates, hormones, organic acids, and antimicrobial compounds. Honey is a good carbohydrate source and supplies energy at 63 calories per tablespoon. It is a rich storehouse of essential vitamins, minerals and trace elements.

Vitamin and Mineral Content of Honey

Vitamin a
Betacarotene
B-complex vitamins (complete)
Vitamin C
Vitamin D
Vitamin E
Vitamin K
Magnesium
Sulfur
Phosphorus
Iron
Calcium
Chlorine
Potassium
Iodine
Sodium
Copper
Manganese

NOTE: Raw honey contains a rich supply of live enzymes which are required for the proper functioning of all body systems. Like royal jelly, bee pollen and propolis, some substances in honey cannot be identified, hence they cannot be chemically reproduced.

CHARACTER: antibiotic, antiviral, anti-inflammatory, anti-carcinogenic, expectorant, anti-allergenic, laxative, anti-anemic, tonic

BODY SYSTEMS TARGETED: Intestinal, Integumentary, Skeletal, (Tonic to all systems)

FORMS: Honey is available in a variety of forms including the following:

Liquid: This type of honey is extracted from the honeycomb through centrifugal force or straining. It is the most common form of honey sold in the U.S. and should be free of visible crystallization. Some forms of liquid honey will contain a part of the cut honeycomb.

Creamed: Creamed honey is crystallized honey. This form of honey comes in a spreadable form and is usually a milky white color.

Comb Honey: This form of honey is still contained in its original honey-comb which can be also eaten or chewed.

Storing Tips

Honey should be stored at room temperature. In time, even liquid Honey will begin to form crystals. Honey crystals can be dissolved by either micro waving the Honey on high for two minutes or placing it in a double boiler and heating.

MEDICINAL APPLICATIONS OF HONEY

Honey: The Perfect Food

Dr. Paavo O. Airola, author of Health Secrets from Europe has written:

"Honey is a perfect food. It contains large amounts of vitamins, minerals, being particularly rich in vitamins B and C. It contains almost all vitamins of the B-complex, which are needed in the system for the digestion and metabolism of sugar. Honey is also rich in minerals such as calcium, phosphorus, magnesium, potassium, silicon, etc. This is specifically true of the darker varieties, such as buckwheat. The vitamin C content varies considerably, depending on the source of the nectar. Some kinds may contain as much as 300 milligrams of vitamin C per 100 grams of honey."

Honey as a Natural Energizer

For centuries Honey has been used to supply energy and rejuvenate the body. Athletes throughout the world use Honey to increase their reserve of immediate energy. Remember, due to its balanced sugar formula, Honey requires no intermediate steps for proper digestion. For this reason, it is a source of rapidly supplied energy.

"The glycogen in a spoonful of honey is said to pass into the bloodstream in 10 minutes to produce quick energy. If taken with a calcium supplement, the glucose in honey can increase the body's uptake of the mineral by nearly 25 percent."[72]

While many people see Honey as just another form of sugar, it has many advantages over refined, white, table sugar. See an upcoming section for reasons why Honey is superior to sugar.

The Healing Properties of Honey

One very universal application of Honey has been to promote the rapid healing of wounds. Honey is the perfect agent for any kind of injury which involves breaking the skin because it protects against infection while boosting the healing process. A number of clinical studies have recognized the wound healing capacities of unprocessed honey. In some cases, raw Honey was sterilized to ensure that it was free of botulinum organisms. Laboratory tests have confirmed that honey can exert a protective effect against all kinds of abscesses including gastric lesions or ulcers.[73]

French scientists conducted tests investigating the value of Honey as a healing agent, and found that Honey healed 88 percent of 40 patients with wounds of various kinds.[74] They concluded that, "this simple, efficient, cheap and with no side effects treatment deserves being better known and integrated in the set of common antiseptics."[75]

Honey: A Natural Anti-Microbial Agent

More and more research is confirming what the ancients already knew; that Honey has impressive, natural antibiotic and antiseptic properties. Recent research conducted in Nigeria confirmed that Honey does indeed exert antibacterial action on certain pathogens which were causing cases of diarrhea.[76] It is the ability of Honey to stop the proliferation of infection that has made it a traditional treatment for wounds. Today, its antibiotic action is in the process of re-discovery within scientific communities, which are openly expressing their surprise at the important value and potential of Honey as a therapeutic agent.

Ulcer Treatment with Honey

Recent in vitro tests found that Honey exhibited a significant inhibitory effect on the heliocobacter pylori bacteria thought to be the single most common cause of gastric ulcers. These tests found that Honey was better at stopping the action of H. Pylori than several other antimicrobial agents.[77] Their recommendation following the study reads: "Our study advocates carrying out clinical investigations of the effect of Honey on gastroduodenal disorders colonized by H. Pylori."[78]

Respiratory Ailments and Honey

Royden Brown in his Bee Hive Product Bible summarizes the important use of Honey to treat a whole host of respiratory ailments from extensive Bulgarian research:

"We found Honey has bactericidal, anti-allergenic, anti-inflammatory and expectorant properties that insure the body an immunobiological defense and give it the capacity to regenerate its attacked cells. Of 17,862 patients treated with Honey, 8,836 were men and 9,026 were women. Most of the patients ranged from 21 to 60 years old."[79] The results found that honey facilitated improvement in cases of: chronic bronchitis, asthmatic bronchitis, bronchial asthma, chronic rhinitis, allergic rhinitis and sinusitis. The report concluded:

"The treatment of non-specific disease of the air passages with honey is efficient when the right honey type and method are used."[80]

NOTE: Honey should never be used to treat any condition if a sensitivity to honey exists. Anyone who is allergy prone should establish whether they are allergic to Honey before using it therapeutically.

Honey vs. Sugar

Honey is a mixture of glucose and fructose, while white sugar is made up of sucrose. As mentioned earlier, the simple types of sugars found in Honey are more easily assimilated into the bloodstream than the disaccharide form of sugar found in refined cane or beet sugars. In addition, Honey glucose boosts the absorption of essential minerals such as zinc, calcium and magnesium, while ordinary sugar can actually leech these same minerals from the body. Eating white sugar can weaken bones and even block growth by inhibting the amount of calcium absorption in the intestinal system, hence the bones do not receive the calcium they need.

Another advantage Honey has over white sugar is that unlike white sugar, it has not been linked with the development of carcinogens which have been linked to certain types of cancer. The over-secretion of insulin brought on by white sugar consumption has been connected with the formation of carcinogens in the body which may affect organs like the breast.

Another important difference between Honey and sugar is an essential one. Raw Honey can rightfully be considered a living food which contains a whole host of nutrients intrinsic to its natural production by Honeybees. White sugar is a dead substance devoid of vitamins and minerals. The fact that it is badly abused and terribly over consumed in this country is cause for alarm. The human body was not designed to cope with such tremendous amounts of refined sucrose.

An added bonus to using Honey is that you get more sweetening power per tablespoon of Honey than other common sweeteners.

ACTIONS OF HONEY

*increases calcium absorption
*can increase hemoglobin count and treat or prevent anemia caused by nutritional factors
*when combined with vinegar, can help arthritic joints
*fights colds and respiratory infections of all kinds
*when used externally, speeds the healing process
*can help to boost gastrointestinal ulcer healing
*works as a natural and gentle laxative
*provides an array of vitamins and minerals
*supplies instant energy without the insulin surge caused by white sugar

Honey as a Base for Other Supplements

Honey provides the perfect base for other beehive foods like Royal Jelly. It only stands to reason that all beehive products would complement each other, however, Honey offers other advantages as well. For one thing, it serves to preserve and protect the nutrient value and potency of Royal Jelly. In addition, because Royal Jelly is bitter to the taste, Honey provides a nutritious and delicious medium, making unpleasant tasting substances palatable. Nature designed the hive and its foods. What better way to present them for human consumption than together as complementary foods.

ROYAL JELLY, BEE POLLEN AND PROPOLIS: A TRINITY OF HEALTH AND LONGEVITY

Beehive products are clearly the most extraordinary elixirs of nutrient power and therapeutic potential in all of the natural world. Nourishing and medicinal, these remarkable foods heal, nourish and protect. Unquestionably, as a synergistic combination, they should be taken together so as to potentiate their beneficial actions within the human body. Royal Jelly rejuvenates and heals, Bee Pollen energizes and invigorates, Propolis protects and regenerates and Honey nourishes and preserves. The combination of these four beehive products is nothing less than perfect.

Vitamin and mineral-rich, foods from the hive provide human physiology with a complete array of life sustaining compounds. These are complete foods, designed by Mother Nature. Their ingredients cannot be duplicated by any means of science. Known to the ancients for their bounty, they emerge again today, as modern scientists re-discover their miraculous properties and new data supports their intrinsic value.

For centuries, humans used beehive foods for strength, health and longevity as medicinal, cosmetic and age-preventing agents. Today, we struggle with a number of devastating degenerative diseases and potentially fatal infections. Beehive products if used consistently and therapeutically, offer our generation a wealth of health benefits without the dangerous side effects of synthetic drugs. The notion of a natural antibiotic, anti-tumor, immune system booster, complete food should certainly get our attention. This is precisely what beehive products offer us. They are nothing less than a powerhouse of health and healing. Unquestionably, this set of foods made in the hive should be found in every kitchen and become the "buzz" words of health minded people everywhere.

FOOTNOTES

[1] Reynard Allen, N.D. and John B. Lust, N.D. The Royal Jelly Miracle. (New York: Benedict Lust Publications, 1958), 2.

[2] Royden Brown. Beehive Product Bible. (New York: Avery Publishing Group, 1993), 108.

[3] Steve Schechter, N.D. "Royal Jelly Handout," (Steven R. Schechter, N.D., 1995), 2. See also S. Barker, Nature, 1959: 183: 199, M. Hoyt. The World of Bees. (New York: Bonanza Books, 1965) and P. Morko. Nature, 1964: 202:188.

[4] Allen, 5.

[5] Schechter, "Royal Jelly," 1.

[6] Brown, 104.

[7] A. Roger, N. Rubira, et. al. "Anaphylaxis caused by royal jelly," Allergol-Immunopathology. 1995: May-June, 23(3): 133-35.

[8] Brown, 111-113.

[9] Carlson Wade. Health From the Hive. (New Canaan, Connecticut: Keats Publishing, 1992), 142.

[10] James A. Devlin, Ph.D. To Your Best Health Naturally. (Prescott, Arizona: Hohm Press, 1994), 137.

[11] Wade, Health From the Hive, 130.

[12] Wade, Health From the Hive, 152.

[13] Devlin, 142.

[14] P.G, Xiao, S.T. Xing and L.W. Wang. "Immunological aspects of Chinese medicinal plants as anti-aging drugs." Journal of Ethnopharmacology. 1993: March 38 (2-3): 167-75.

[15] "Royal Jelly: Health Through Nature." Let's Live Magazine. March, 1990.

[16] Allen, 19.

[17] Wade, 152.

[18] Devlin, 141.

[19] Devlin, 139.

[20] J. Vittek. "Effect of royal jelly on serum lipids in experimental animals and humans with atherosclerosis." Experientia. 1995: Sept. 29 51 (9-10): 927-35.

[21] Ibid.

[22] Alma E. Guiness, ed. Family Guide to Natural Medicine. (New York: The

Reader's Digest Association, 1993), 310.

[23] Devlin, 143-44.

[24] Brown, x.

[25] Ibid., 40.

[26] Ibid., 44.

[27] Wade, 52

[28] Ibid., 53.

[29] Ibid., 58.

[30] Steven, R. Schechter, N.D. "Bee Pollen Handout." (1995, Steven R. Schechter, N.D.), 1.

[31] Ibid.

[32] Schechter, "Bee Pollen Handout," 2.

[33] Ibid.

[34] Schechter, "Bee Pollen Handout," 2. See also Murray L. Maurer and Margaret Strauss. "A New Oral Treatment for Ragweed Fever." Journal of Allergy. 1961: 32:343, Louis Sternberg, "Seasonal Somnolence as Possible Pollen Allergy." Journal of Allergy. V.14, 1942: 89, and J.H. Black. Journal of Chem Med. Vol. 8, May, 1928: 709.

[35] Brown, 44.

[36] Wade, 37.

[37] Ibid., 22.

[38] Ibid, 45.

[39] Carlson Wade. Propolis:Nature's Energizer. (New Canaan, Connecticut: Keats Publishing, 1983), 4.

[40] Ibid.

[41] Devlin, 115.

[42] Wade, Propolis: Nature's Energizer, 5.

[43] Steven R. Schechter, N.D. "Bee Propolis Handout." (1995, Steven R. Schechter, N.D.), 1

[44] Paavo Airola. Are You Confused? (Health Plus Publishers, 1974), 161.

[45] Wade, Propolis: Nature's Energizer, 7.

[46] Devlin, 116.

[47] C.V. Rao, D. Desai, B. Kaul et al. "Effect of caffeic acid esters on carcinogen-induced mutagenicity and human colon adenocarcinoma cell growth." Chemical-Biological Interaction. 1992: Nov. 16 84 (3): 277-90.

[48] Wade, Health From the Hive, 101.

[49] J. Focht, S.H. Hansen, et al. "Bacteriocidal effect of propolis in vitro

against agents causing upper respiratory tract infections."
Arzneimittelforschung. 1993: Aug 43 (8): 921-23.

[50]Wade, Propolis: Nature's Energizer, 7.

[51]K.A. Kuzmina. Therapy with Bee Honey. (Russia: Saratov, 1971).

[52]V.P. Kivalkina. Propolis: Its Antibacterial and Therapeutic Properties.
(Russia: Kasan Publishing Co., 1978).

American Chiropractor. 1979: Feb. Vol.2 No.2.

[54]Kuzima. Therapy with Bee Honey.

[55]Devlin, 116.

[56]Wade, Health From the Hive, 109.

[57]Schechter, "Bee Propolis Handout," 2. See also F.C. Prochum and A.J.
Borovaja. "Bacteriocidal Effects of Propolis and Its Use in Clinical Practice.
Military Medical Journal. 1970 nor. 9, 65.

[58]Brown, 88.

[59]F.D. Makarov. Propolis Therapy, The Healing Art. (Russia: no. 4).

[60]G.F. Zabelina. Propolis (a thesis delivered at K.A. Rachfuss Children's
Hospital, Russia.

[61]Devlin, 119.

[62]Brown, 89.

[63]Ibid.

[64]Ibid., 90.

[65]Ibid., 9.

[66]Rao, 277-90.

[67]Brown, 8.

[68]Globe. March 24, 1980, 5.

[69]Devlin, 115.

[70]Wade, Health From the Hive, 10.

[71]Brown, 127.

[72]Wade, Health From the Hive, 20.

[73]E.F. Elbagoury and S. Rasmy. "Antibacterial action of natural honey on
anaerobic bacteroides." Journal of Egyptian Dentistry. 1993 January: 39
(1): 381- 86.

[74]G. Ndayisaba, L. Bazira and E. Haboniman. "Treatment of Wounds with
honey." Presse-Med. 1992 Oct. 3: 21 (32): 1516-8.

[75]Ibid.

[76]C.L. Obi, E.O. Ugoji, et al. "The antibacterial effect of honey on diarrhea
causing bacterial agents isolated in Lagos, Nigeria." African Journal of

Medical Science. 1994 Sept: 23 (3): 257-60.
[77]A.T. Ali, M.N. Chowdhury, et al. "Inhibitory effect of natural honey on Helicobacter pylori." Trop-Gastroenterology. 1991 Jul-Sept: 12 (3): 139-43.
[78]Ibid.
[79]Brown, 128
[80] Ibid.